Original title:
Ripples of the Tidal Dream

Copyright © 2025 Creative Arts Management OÜ
All rights reserved.

Author: Samuel Kensington
ISBN HARDBACK: 978-1-80587-404-1
ISBN PAPERBACK: 978-1-80587-874-2

The Whisper of the Current

In the waters a frog made a splash,
He jumped too high, oh what a crash!
A fish swam by, with a wink and a grin,
"Watch your bounce! You're in for a spin!"

The turtle slow, with a shell of a seat,
Said, "Life's a race, but don't use your feet!"
"Glide on the waves, let the tide do the rest,
And enjoy your journey, take it with zest!"

Patterns of Serenity

The jellyfish danced with a quirk and a twirl,
Stinging the air, oh what a swirl!
A starfish chimed in with a lazy wave,
"I just chill here, I'm not one to brave!"

The seahorses chuckled, their tails in a knot,
"You never know when you might need a spot!"
They spun in the currents, with joy to be free,
Creating patterns as fun as can be!

Nymphs of the Deep

Bubbles giggled, a bubbly bunch,
While seaweed swayed, enjoying its lunch.
Mermaids chortled, with laughter like bells,
"Don't take life too seriously, just tell fishy tales!"

They played a game of tag with the tides,
Flipping and flopping, oh what a ride!
With waves of humor washing ashore,
Each day a new joke, who could ask for more?

Flowing Possibilities

An otter slipped on a rock, what a sight!
He tumbled and giggled, it filled up the night.
"I meant to do that!" he called with a grin,
"Water's just laughter, let the fun begin!"

The crabs clapped claws in a joyous display,
"Come join our feast, there's plenty to play!"
With snacks from the sea, and jokes from the shore,
Life in the deep is never a bore!

Dancing Currents

In the ocean's disco ball, they twirl,
Fins flapping wildly, giving a whirl.
Clams clap their shells, keeping the beat,
While starfish groove with lazy little feet.

Jellyfish float in a wobbly row,
With squishy moves, they steal the show.
Crabs catch the rhythm, side-to-side,
Underwater parties, a slippery ride.

Tides of Reflection

Waves crash like laughter on sandy shores,
As seagulls gossip and tumble outdoors.
Sandcastles topple with a giggly crash,
While kids run wild in a colorful splash.

A whale tells jokes with a deep belly laugh,
While dolphins practice their finest giraffe.
Starfish snicker, they hide up their sleeves,
As the current tickles the sand's little leaves.

Moonlit Movements

Under the moon, the fish start to dance,
With bubbles of laughter, they jump at a chance.
Otters glide down on a silvery slide,
While turtles shake shells with smiles open wide.

The owl hoots softly, it's time for a jest,
As otters play tag in their cozy nest.
A crab spins around in its fanciest shoe,
While the night's gentle breeze whispers, 'Who knew?'

Undercurrents of Thought

Beneath the surface, ideas take flight,
With seaweed scribbling, they write day and night.
Octopus scribbles with ink on a shell,
While fish share secrets, oh what a swell!

Thoughts drift like bubbles, some rise, some sink,
As sea cucumbers stop to giggle and think.
Brain coral whispers, wise beyond years,
While laughter erupts, louder than cheers.

Tide Pools of Memory

In pools of water, laughter sways,
Forgotten thoughts in sandy bays.
Crabby critters, quite a show,
Pinching toes, oh how they flow!

A starfish giggles, tales it spins,
With seaweed wigs, it surely wins.
Seashells whisper jokes from long ago,
Echoing waves, a funny flow!

Jellyfish bounce in silly grace,
While minnows dance, a speedy race.
Their fins tickle like playful nuns,
In tide pools where the fun just runs!

When sunsets paint the ocean gold,
The memories drift, a sight to behold.
Laughter lingers in each splash,
As dreams of tide pools make a splash!

Shadows of the Surf

The shadows stretch, the surf does laugh,
A wave recites, a silly gaffe.
With boogie boards in tow, they ride,
While seagulls cackle, oh what pride!

Surfboards wobble, caught in gleam,
Chasing shadows that dance and dream.
A hermit crab in flip-flop shoes,
Struts along with royal clues!

Mermaids giggle, crowns askew,
In foamy curls, they join the queue.
The ocean's jest, a playful swirl,
As sandy toes begin to twirl!

Beneath the sun, where shadows prance,
Laughter echoes, a joyful dance.
The surf's embrace, a gentle tease,
In waves of fun, we find our ease!

Fluid Horizons

Horizons stretch in hues of play,
Where silly thoughts just drift away.
A dolphin dons a bowler hat,
And makes a splash—imagine that!

With sea cucumbers grooving slow,
They twist and twirl, a fluid show.
The ocean sings a tune of cheer,
As barnacles plot their next career!

A pelican prances, flapping wide,
Trying to surf on a jelly tide.
While fish in slippers take a stroll,
In fluid dreams, they reach their goal!

The sunset blends, a wacky sight,
Where giggles dance with fading light.
In every splash and silly dive,
Fluid horizons keep the fun alive!

Dancing with the Deep

The deep sea calls with laughter bright,
As creatures twirl in playful flight.
A fish with flair and painted face,
Convinces octopus to join the race!

With bubbles bursting, jokes are told,
As eels slip by with wiggles bold.
A turtle's hat, quite out of style,
Wears fashion sense with goofy smiles!

Coral blooms in colors loud,
Where every fish is proud and cowed.
They dance beneath the waves of glee,
Embracing life in harmony!

As currents swirl in whimsical beat,
We laugh along, no chance of defeat.
In the deep, where dreams collide,
We find our fun, and joy abides!

Dreams in Driftwood

On a beach where sea-logs lay,
They told me tales of yesterday.
A crab in a hat sang a tune,
Beneath the light of a laughing moon.

The seagulls danced a jolly jig,
While starfish played a tiny gig.
A whale wore glasses, quite a sight,
Sipping lemonade, feeling light.

Octopuses tangled in a mess,
Playing cards in a game of chess.
The tide brought whispers of the past,
As jellyfish floated, oh so fast.

Amidst the sands, the stories swell,
In driftwood dreams, all is well.
So let the laughter fill the air,
For who knows what magic's lurking there!

Tracing the Shoreline

Footprints lead the way in lines,
Sketches made by wandering minds.
A shrimp took up a quirky pose,
As waves tickled its little toes.

The sandcastles had their own flair,
With turrets built without a care.
Seashells whispered gossip galore,
About the fish who opened a store.

Crabs in tuxedos strutted proud,
Their tiny audience, a laughing crowd.
The horizon wore a vibrant shirt,
Making the sunset seem absurdly curt.

Drawing maps with the tide's embrace,
Every wave a new hiding place.
So grab a shovel, dig with glee,
As you trace laughter along the sea!

Melodies Beneath the Surface

Bubbles rise with a silly sound,
Like fish singing all around.
A guppy played a tiny flute,
While clams grooved in vibrant suits.

Anemones wiggled to the beat,
With sea urchins tapping their feet.
Tadpoles joined in with a splash,
As dolphins twirled in a briny flash.

The currents played a whimsical song,
As underwater friends danced along.
A treasure chest groaned with delight,
When seahorses took flight that night.

And if you listen with open ears,
You'll find laughter hidden in tears.
For the ocean hums a silly tune,
Under the gaze of a cheeky moon!

The Language of the Ocean

The waves whispered secrets to the shore,
With giggles that echoed more and more.
A pelican shared a fishy joke,
As washouts laughed and nearly spoke.

Barnacles pondered the meaning of fun,
While sailing boats aimed for the sun.
Crabs and clams held a debate,
On whether it's better to swim or skate.

The tide rolled in, a playful sigh,
As dolphins leapt for the starry sky.
Each splash a word, each wave a laugh,
In the ocean's great fun-loving path.

So next time you're strolling by the sea,
Listen closely; maybe you'll see.
The language of laughter, wide and free,
In every drop from the wild, vast sea!

Of Shells and Stars

A shell lay on the sandy shore,
It whispered tales of ocean's lore.
A starfish danced, quite out of tune,
Trying hard to woo the moon.

The crabs all laughed from their small piles,
While fish swam by with silly smiles.
They sang a song of seaweed hair,
And joked about the surfer's scare.

A dolphin juggled sea grapes high,
While seagulls cheered from way up high.
With each splash, a giggle came,
As jellyfish joined in the game.

In this wavy party so divine,
The sea's a stage where all align.
A slapstick show on ocean's floor,
Where shells and stars could ask for more!

Mysteries of the Deep Blue

A fish in stripes wore polka dots,
Claiming to be a dancing spot.
The octopus, with eight left feet,
Tried a jig that couldn't compete.

A crab held court with comical glee,
In a shell-shaped throne, sipping briny tea.
Mermaids giggled at their own reflection,
While whales wrote notes with perfect projection.

With every wave, a new tall tale,
Of treasures lost or ships that sail.
They tossed a beach ball made of fluff,
And laughed hard when the tide got tough.

In deep blue realms where humor thrives,
The ocean waves keep all alive.
Every splash, a fresh surprise,
Amidst the glee, the laughter flies.

Choreography of the Waves

The waves perform a dance so grand,
With fish in flippers, it's all unplanned.
A seal spins round, then takes a bow,
While dolphins leap and eat a cow!

From sandy stage, the starfish cheer,
Each splash reverberates with glee here.
A sandy surfer wipes out at last,
His dance now joined—by all amassed!

The gulls chirp tunes, they're quite a band,
With shells as instruments, oh so grand.
The rhythm shifts, the tempo grows,
Each wave a step, each tide a show.

So let the ocean lead the way,
With smiles and laughter on display.
In nature's theater, wild and free,
The choreography brings pure glee.

Fables from the Foam

In foamy tales of yonder seas,
A clam spun yarns with clammy knees.
He said, 'I saw a ship go by,
With pirates who thought they could all fly!'

There once was a frog, or so they claim,
Who fancied himself a surfing fame.
With a tiny board and a giant wave,
He landed hard, yet he was brave!

A walrus told of jellybeans,
That grew on rocks and were bright green.
The other critters laughed so hard,
They rolled around, their joy unmarred.

So gather 'round the ocean's edge,
For fables full of humor's pledge.
From every splash and foam-filled spree,
An endless joke lives wild and free!

Sublime Undercurrents of Thought

In the ocean's mind, fish wear hats,
While seagulls dance with ballet mats.
A crab recites Shakespeare, oh so grand,
While starfish form a rock band.

Waves whisper secrets, tickling the sand,
A jellyfish waltzes, unplanned.
Sea cucumbers giggle, turning to greet,
As dolphins hold a conga beat.

Mermaids sip tea, plotting their schemes,
As octopuses sketch their wild dreams.
In this underwater ball of mirth,
They ponder the meaning and silliness of birth.

Oh, bubbles of laughter rise in the swell,
With every splash, they giggle and yell.
Where fishy thoughts flow, there's joy in the tide,
In this charming realm, the weirdos reside.

Mists of Enchantment on the Shore

At dawn's first light, a clam sings tunes,
While crabs sip lattes by the dunes.
Seahorses strut in their best bow ties,
As gulls debate the heights of the skies.

A beach ball floats with a wise, old crab,
Revealing secrets most would nab.
Waves tickle toes in a playful spree,
As shells caper under the sun's decree.

Sandcastles rise, with moats of delight,
While children laugh, what a sight!
Parents, sprawled like basking seals,
Find joy in depths of silly ideals.

In misty enchantment, all feels surreal,
As the tide gently tickles each heel.
The sun winks knowingly, sharing its beams,
Making every grain sing glittering dreams.

The Journey of Drifting Dreams

On a wave of whimsy, dreams set sail,
With jellybeans trailing a candy trail.
A fish in pajamas flips through the air,
While mermaids giggle without a care.

Seashells gossip, exchanging old tales,
Of pirates who tripped on their own sails.
A narwhal wears a party hat,
As dolphins play leapfrog, imagine that!

Floating along on this bright, cheery tide,
With laughter and mischief, we'll glide.
A feast of seaweed and coral pie,
Where everyone dances; oh my, oh my!

As dreams drift forth in this vibrant sphere,
Each twist, each turn, brings good cheer.
With silly antics amidst ocean's sway,
We feel the joy in each playful spray.

A Symphony of Glimmering Depths

In the siren's song, there's giggling delight,
With fishy puns that sparkle so bright.
A clam conductor waves its shell in time,
While seaweed sways in rhythm and rhyme.

Turtles tap dance, spinning in glee,
Teaching the minnow how to belly free.
Anemones tickle, and bubbles pop loud,
As the sea hosts a merry crowd.

A symphony of laughter floats through the blue,
With squid on saxophones, playing anew.
Crabs with their castanets keep the beat,
While clownfish somersault, not missing a seat.

Echoes of merriment shimmer and shine,
Tickling the senses, so divine!
In the depths of the sea, there's a joyful spree,
Creating a harmony that's bound to be free.

The Language of Swelling Waters

When waves start to chat, oh what a sound,
They gossip and laugh, all around the ground.
Salty jokes they spin, from shore to shore,
Making fish chuckle, then beg for more.

Seaweed dances, twirls in the breeze,
Shimmering jokes passed 'round with such ease.
Crabs cracking up, they pinch with delight,
As the ocean spills secrets all through the night.

Bubbles rise up, with giggles so light,
Tickling the shores, a comical sight.
Seashells join in, with their wisdom to share,
Chortling and chuckling, without any care.

So dive in the laughter, let currents ignite,
Join the frolicsome waves, in pure oceanic light.
For in every splash, and wave's joyful leap,
Lies humor and fun, in the deep and the steep.

Dreams Carried by Floating Leaves

Leaves on the river, they chatter and glide,
They tickle the water, with zany pride.
Whispering tales of the sun's silly grin,
As ducks quack along, with a laugh from within.

A leaf wears a hat, made of dew and sun,
Floating like a boat, oh what a fun run!
Fish peek from below, with eyes wide and bright,
Wondering if leaves have parties each night.

The current throws jokes, like floaties on air,
Splashing with laughter, a whimsical flair.
And when the wind howls, it sings a new tune,
Picture leaves dancing under a bright, silly moon.

So join in the mirth, let your worries release,
For on this leaf voyage, there's nothing but peace.
With giggles and wiggles, we laugh and we weave,
As we sail down the stream with dreams on a leave.

Harmonies of the Deep Blue

In the sea's orchestra, the fish play the strings,
They strum on the water, oh what joy it brings.
Songs rise like bubbles, tickling the foam,
As laughter resounds through their watery home.

A whale hums bass, with a belly so grand,
While dolphins provide a whimsical band.
Crabs clap their claws, adding beats with flair,
Creating a concert, an aquatic fair.

The coral chimes in, with colors so bright,
Painting the sea floor in a musical light.
Starfish pair dance, in elegant twirls,
Spreading laughter outwards, like underwater pearls.

So join in the chorus, let your heart sway,
In the symphony of laughter, come out and play.
For in these deep waters, where fun intertwines,
Every wave holds a note, where humor shines.

The Pull of Celestial Strings

Stars twinkle above, like giggles in space,
Pulling at oceans, causing a wiggly race.
The moon's a jester, playing with tides,
While comets create splashes, as laughter collides.

The sun cracks a smile, igniting the day,
Casting shadows that dance in a playful way.
Seashells sing softly, with songs full of cheer,
As the universe chuckles, drawing us near.

Galaxies whirl, in a dizzying spin,
While starfish chuckle, with winsome grins.
Cosmic humor flows, through the vastness of night,
In the hands of the heavens, what a glorious sight!

So reach for the stars, let your heart take flight,
For laughter's a wave, in the vast blue so bright.
In the pull of the cosmos, we twirl and we sway,
Finding joy in the journey, come join the play!

Waves of Whimsy

In the ocean's laugh so bright,
Fish wear hats, what a sight!
Jellybeans dance on foamy waves,
Every fish is a prankster, it braves.

Seahorses trot with a comical pride,
Octopuses juggle, their arms spread wide!
Clownfish giggle in coral caves,
They tickle sea turtles and make them crave.

Stars in the sky envy the show,
Seashells clink as they join the flow.
Life under waves is quite the jest,
In silly antics, fish are the best!

With every splash, joy finds its way,
Laughter bubbles up, come what may.
A whimsical world, we can't ignore,
Where every wave calls for a roar!

Currents of Hope

Bubbles rise with dreams afloat,
A lonely shark rides on a boat.
He plans a race with fish so spry,
But undersea, it's hard to fly.

Turtles wear shades, trying to be cool,
While sea cucumbers flop, acting the fool.
Hope glides through like a dolphin queen,
In a buoyant world, life's a zany scene.

Glimmers of laughter spark with delight,
As fish tell tales in the moonlight.
They hope for snacks from above, it's clear,
The currents of joy always draw near.

A treasure chest spills out with fun,
Filled with giggles, not just sun.
In the deep blue, hopes find their way,
With laughter, we splash through the day!

Journeys in the Undersea

With a snorkel on and fins so bright,
Crabs cartwheel in pure delight.
Every wave brings a silly song,
In the undersea, nothing feels wrong.

Burbling shrimp have a dance to share,
They pull in friends from everywhere.
A wobbly whale starts a conga line,
While sea anemones sway and shine.

Starfish snap selfies on the seafloor,
A tale of mischief, oh what a score!
They giggle and play with every tide,
On this journey, joy is our guide.

The deep sea's whimsy is truly grand,
Where laughter flows through the ocean's hand.
With every swim, adventures unfurl,
In a world where silly dreams twirl.

Fleeting Moments

With every splash, a memory made,
Little fish dance in their parade.
Seagulls swoop and join the fun,
In fleeting moments, joy's never done.

A crab in a tux makes quite the scene,
While clams do the cha-cha, they're rather keen.
Winking shells tell secrets from wide,
In the sea of laughter, we take pride.

Every moment, a burst of glee,
As dolphins race through with giddy spree.
Who knew the ocean could be so bright?
With fleeting laughs that take flight!

Bubbles pop, the fun won't cease,
In the tidal giggles, we find our peace.
Cherish the laughter, it's a treasure true,
In every wave, there's joy anew!

Subtle Undulations

The ocean danced with a wink,
Fish wore sunglasses, took a drink.
Seagulls laughed as they swooped low,
Tickling waves like a splashy show.

Crabs tap-danced on sandy floors,
Jellyfish played in their translucent shores.
With every wave, a joke was thrown,
A splash of humor, brightly grown.

Shells recited rhymes in delight,
While starfish twirled in a moonlit night.
A seahorse stole the seashell stage,
As laughter echoed from page to page.

The tide knew how to keep it light,
With every splash, it took to flight.
Waves snickered, the surf tickled toes,
In this grand play, everyone knows.

The Heartbeat of the Sea

With each wave, the ocean chuckles,
As crabs make plans and jellyfish snuggle.
A starfish flips in a great big swirl,
While seaweed dances, giving a twirl.

Octopuses tango in polka-dot shoes,
While dolphins giggle, spreading their muse.
The ocean's heart beats with a grin,
Tickling the shore as the fun begins.

Clams keep secrets, shells tell tales,
A medley of humor in the salty gales.
Waves whisper jokes to the boats afloat,
As the tide writes laughter, a rhythmic note.

In each current, joy rides the breeze,
Water's heartbeat brings us to our knees.
With swells of laughter, the sea does play,
In this funny world, we splash away.

Fractals of Light

Beneath the waves, colors collide,
Like a disco party, they swiftly glide.
Fish wear costumes, glittering bright,
Fractals of laughter in beams of light.

A clownfish juggles, what a sight,
While sea turtles bicker, just for spite.
Anemones wave in giddy delight,
As bubbles pop with jokes in flight.

Sunbeams tickle the ocean's face,
Creating a stage for the sea's embrace.
The coral reef hums a funny tune,
While starfish argue who's got the best prunes.

In the swell of humor, we find our place,
As every wave wears a joyful face.
The ocean's pulse is a laughter spree,
Painting each moment in glee and glee.

Silk and Salt

The sea's a tailor; stitching up fun,
With silk and salt, it's never done.
Waves roll like fabric, smooth and grand,
Dressed in laughter, hand in hand.

Fish in tuxedos swim here and there,
Laughing as they comb through the air.
A manta rays' dance, oh what a spree!
Silk, salt, and sunshine, wild and free.

Tidal waves twirl with a wink and a nod,
While starfish spin; they're the stars of the odd.
Crabs grumble softly about their attire,
While seagulls play trumpets, lifting spirits higher.

With every wave, a fresh jest is sewn,
In this sea wardrobe, we're never alone.
So raise a glass to the tides, my friend,
In this goofy ocean, the fun never ends.

Translucent Paths of Unseen Currents

In the water, fishes dance,
Chasing bubbles, what a chance!
A turtle grins, winking bright,
As crabs hold a spotlight fight.

A clam plays hide and seek with flair,
While seahorses spin in midair.
Jellyfish float like quirky kites,
As octopuses tag with their lights.

Anemones wave like busy hands,
As starfish mess with ocean bands.
Mermaids giggle at the show,
As barnacles steal the limelight glow.

The waves clap their foamy cheer,
Underwater laughs fill clear.
Who knew the sea had such glee?
Oh, come join the aquatic spree!

Embraced by the Sea's Sigh

A dolphin slips with a devilish grin,
Splashing humans, where to begin?
They laugh and scream, it's quite the sight,
As seagulls squawk, joining the fight.

A fish in a bowler hat swims by,
Proposing a dance in the salty sky.
Starfish twirl in their best attire,
While the clam plays tunes with shells that inspire.

The seaweed sways like it's at a ball,
Inviting all creatures, both big and small.
Crustaceans groove as they tap their claws,
While sea cucumbers simply pause.

The whispers of waves tell jokes so grand,
In this underwater, silliness land.
Under the sea where fun's always high,
Even the fish occasionally sigh!

Horizons Whispered in Salty Breezes

On sandy shores, laughter unfolds,
With jellybeans washing, new tales told.
A crab in a hat, proud as can be,
Sells lemonade, take a sip, just for free!

The gulls squawk puns with raucous delight,
As children chase waves, what a sight!
Sandcastles rise like grand hotels,
While the tide sneaks in—oh, who can tell?

A flip-flop flings at a nearby seal,
As beach balls bounce with zestful zeal.
A sunburned pirate shows off his tan,
Dancing a jig, much to the clan.

The horizon giggles with colors so bright,
As the sun dips down, wrapping up light.
In salty breezes, joy is released,
This coastal comedy never ceased!

The Ever-Changing Canvas of Night

The stars come out for a wacky show,
With constellations putting on a glow.
An owl with glasses reads the sky,
While fireflies mock the moon up high.

Waves whisper secrets to the crickets' tune,
As nocturnal critters hold a balloon.
A raccoon juggles shiny rocks,
While frogs croak out the latest talks.

The night brings laughter, endless and bright,
Creatures dance under the silver light.
A sleepy land where dreams take flight,
In this quirky space, all feels just right.

The canvas shifts, painted in glee,
With a dash of fun from the old oak tree.
Each glimmering echo, a joyful sound,
As the ocean joins in, laughter abound.

The Depths of Desire

In the sea of my thoughts, fish wear hats,
They dance and they prance, oh how they chat.
Octopuses juggle, a crab's stuck in a pose,
While seahorses giggle, with tickles on toes.

A dolphin named Dave, he thinks he's so slick,
He tells all his tales with a funny little flick.
But when he tries diving, he comes up with flair,
Waving his fins, like he's teasing the air.

A clam wrote a poem, but it's full of bad puns,
About sand and the beach and a race with the buns.
With every new line, a new wave of glee,
Even the sharks join in, singing off-key.

So beneath the blue waves, in this curious place,
Fish jest in the tides, with laughter and grace.
The depths of desire, in this silly parade,
Life's a splashy joke, in a finny charade.

Flowing Whispers

Whispers of bubbles, they giggle and pop,
A starfish named Larry, he can't seem to stop.
He tickles a turtle, who laughs with delight,
Dancing with jellyfish through the long moonlit night.

The current flows softly, like a tickle on skin,
A seaweed ballet where the fun can begin.
A clam offers shells, as hats for the fish,
They prance in the currents, that's their only wish.

An eel tells a joke, but it's quite a long line,
The fish roll their eyes, and say, "Oh, that's fine!"
The waves are alive, and the laughter ignites,
Funny fish parties, oh, what silly sights!

So follow the whispers, let giggles cascade,
In the depths of the ocean, where joy won't fade.
The flowing laughter will linger and flow,
In this underwater joke, we rake in the glow.

Whirls of Wonder

In a whirlpool of giggles, a fish slips and slides,
A clownfish named Freddy, in his polka dot rides.
He twirls and he turns, what a sight to behold,
With each splash of color, his stories unfold.

A seagull swoops down, with a cheeky old grin,
He wants to join in, but flops on the skin.
The fish all break out into rippling cheer,
"Join us, oh birdie, come shake off your fear!"

The dolphins are laughing, jumping high in the air,
Waving their tails, with nary a care.
As the ocean spins round, in a whirl of delight,
All nature's a stage, on this fun-filled night.

So dive in, take a chance, don't let life just ponder,
In these whirls of wonder, let your laughter wander.
With fins and with flippers, let the fun take flight,
In the ocean's embrace, everything feels right.

A Distant Horizon

Beyond the horizon, where the silly waves play,
A fish with a mustache leads the way to sway.
With sunglasses so cool and a wide, goofy grin,
He tells of adventures, where the wild things spin.

A mermaid with sparkles joins in for the ride,
Her laughter like bubbles, she feels quite the pride.
They build castles of sand, but they keep falling down,
The octopus grins, and says, "You're a clown!"

From distant horizons, the laughter does soar,
With every new wave, there's a chuckle in store.
The sun's a big joker, as it sets with a show,
Painting the skies with a vibrant, bright glow.

So come, take the plunge, let your laughter be wide,
In this whimsical journey, let your heart be your guide.
In the playful embrace of the ocean's vast scene,
You'll find joy forever, as light as a dream.

Cascading Reflections on Water

In the pond, a frog leaps high,
Splashing down, oh my, oh my!
He blinks at fish with bulging eyes,
The tadpoles giggle, oh, what a prize!

Ducks parade in silly lines,
Waddling around, oh how it shines!
One quacks loud, a comic sound,
The others chuckle, joy is found!

A boat floats by, a man with snacks,
He drops a chip, the ducks attack!
Chaos reigns, and laughter swells,
As crumbs transform to swimming spells!

Nature's stage, a comedy play,
Silly moments, bright as day!
With every splash, a spark ignites,
Life's little joys, oh what delights!

A Serenade to the Shifting Sands

On the beach, seagulls strut,
Dancing 'round a peanut nut!
A group of crabs holds a debate,
About which way to scuttle straight!

A child builds a castle tall,
Only to watch it tumble and fall!
He laughs and shrieks, 'What a show!'
The tide rolls in, 'Oh no, oh no!'

The sunburned dad applies his cream,
Misses spots, it's quite the scene!
His wife just laughs, what a sight!
Shining like a beacon, oh what delight!

Footprints dance in the shimmering sand,
As laughter echoes across the strand!
A day like this, who could resist?
The shifting sands, a funny twist!

Beyond the Horizon's Embrace

A pirate ship sails into the blue,
With a parrot who sings, 'Cuckoo, cuckoo!'
The captain sneezes, 'Ah-choo, ah-choo!'
The crew erupts, 'Is that your cue?'

At sunset, the sky blushes bright,
Waves slap the hull, oh what a sight!
The crew plays cards with jellyfish,
Who keeps on winning, what a wish!

A whale splashes, flips with flair,
The shipmates gasp, but don't despair!
'He's just showing off,' the captain grins,
As they sail on, with squeals and sins!

Across the ocean, laughter sails,
In every breeze, adventure hails!
A horizon painted in hues so bold,
With stories of laughter forever told!

Fluid Echoes of the Night

The moon peeks out, a curious chap,
Dancing on waves, what a mishap!
Stars giggle softly, twinkling bright,
'We hide and seek, till morning light!'

A fish jumps high, in a silver arc,
'Did you see that?' quips a shark.
But as he boasts, he loses grip,
And flops right back, became a blip!

Crickets serenade with a hum,
As the fireflies twirl, oh here they come!
They rush and swirl, in a joyous flight,
Drawing doodles in the depths of night!

Laughter bubbles, even the breeze,
Join the fun, with such great ease!
In fluid echoes, tales unwind,
Of silly antics, that humor binds!

Sounds of the Deep

Bubbles pop and fish do sing,
A turtle tiptoes, wearing bling.
Seaweed dances, swaying tall,
As crabs play chess beneath the sprawl.

Jellyfish float like disco balls,
While dolphins giggle through the halls.
Starfish wave, with countless arms,
In the ocean's school of silly charms.

Octopus juggles shells so bright,
Comedic bends in moonlit night.
Seahorses trot on tiny legs,
Waving to clams that sound like pegs.

The deep sea's laughter never ends,
With whirlpool spins where time transcends.
A watery world of joke and cheer,
Where each splash says, "Come over here!"

Veils of the Vortex

In the swirl where whirlpools dance,
A seagull strutted, took a chance.
Caught in the spin, a fish did zomp,
With sea-salt hair, just like a pomp.

An octopus with socks of pink,
Bobbing in bubbles, made us think.
While eels joked, tangled in a twist,
Said, "Brush your teeth, you shouldn't miss!"

Mermaids giggle, toss their hair,
In this vortex—it's quite the scare!
But laughter bubbles from the foam,
As they splash in their briny home.

Dolphins leap, and krill they tease,
"Watch us glide with such great ease!"
The whirlpool giggles, makes a fuss,
In the vortex, it's all a plus!

Echoes on the Wind

Seagulls chime in, squawking loud,
Telling tales of fishy crowds.
Whales whistle, their tuneful call,
Echoes bouncing, we have a ball.

The breeze carries laughter, oh so sweet,
Mermaids play tag with quick little feet.
Crabs on the shore tap their claws,
Creating a band—now clap, applause!

Jellyfish dance, floating with glee,
Tickling the sea, where all is free.
The wind whispers, blowing a tune,
Dancing and singing beneath the moon.

With each gust, the tales expand,
Of underwater fun, oh so grand.
On breezy waves, with giggles to send,
Each echo shared, like notes to mend.

Remnants of the Current

Currents swirl like a giant trick,
Carrying swimmers in a playful flick.
Snails use surfboards, racing around,
While otters laugh, now don't fall down!

Seashells whispered secrets, quite absurd,
As fish told jokes without a word.
With bubbles popping, laughter flows,
In the currents where everyone knows.

With jellybeans dropped, a sweetened tide,
Fishes giggle as they glide.
The current chuckles—starts a chase,
In a bubbly, fun-filled, fishy race.

Laughter lingers with a splash and dart,
These sea antics warm the heart.
As the waves waddle, glisten, and twirl,
The current waves, "Hey! Who needs a swirl?"

Whispers of the Ocean's Caress

The seagulls squawk with glee,
As waves tickle toes so free.
In bucket hats, we build our walls,
While sandcastles face nature's brawls.

A crab in a tuxedo struts by,
Waving its claws, oh my, oh my!
The tide plays tricks, it's quite absurd,
As flip-flops sail, all without a word.

Salty snacks tossed in the breeze,
As fish throw shade from beneath the seas.
We laugh so hard, we snort a bit,
While jellyfish dance, our fun won't quit.

And as the sun dips low and bright,
We chase the tide with squeals of delight.
The ocean's giggles echo far,
A comical night beneath the star.

Echoes Beneath the Surface

Fish in wigs swim with flair,
Their cool style catches every stare.
In schools they gossip, fins at play,
So much drama beneath the spray.

A dolphin dons a bowler hat,
Chasing bubbles—just like that!
Octopuses juggle shells on a dare,
While sea turtles slow dance with flair.

A treasure chest full of old socks,
Turns into a dance-off by the docks.
Seashells laugh as they strategize,
And clams will roll their googly eyes.

Beneath it all, the fun's quite grand,
A watery world, a playful band.
With bubbles popping like sweet champagne,
The echoes of laughter, our joy's refrain.

The Dance of Moonlit Waves

The moonlight glistens on ocean's face,
As fish put on their disco grace.
A shrimp in shades catches the beat,
While crabs conga along the sheet.

Starfish twirl on the sandy floor,
With wiggly moves we can't ignore.
Shellfish snap a selfie so sly,
With pearls of laughter—they're flying high.

The seaweed sways to a funky tune,
While blowfish groove beneath the moon.
Barnacles cheer, they're quite the fans,
As plankton form the best dance plans.

When dawn peeks in, the fun won't stop,
As waves still dance, ready to swap.
A tidal party that never ends,
With jokes and jests from ocean friends.

Currents of a Distant Reverie

A fish rode in on a surfboard cool,
Claiming the beach is now its school.
With fins held high and scales so bright,
They teach us how to ride the light.

An octopus wears a snorkeling set,
Chasing waves and dogs in a wet duet.
Seagulls laugh at the silly sight,
While beach balls bounce in sheer delight.

The sand, a canvas of footprints galore,
A seaside ballet rehearsed on the shore.
As tides come in, we splash and shout,
With laughter floating, there's no doubt.

The sun dips down, it's time to dream,
As ocean whispers join our team.
What fun we've had, what tales to share,
In currents where joy floats through the air.

Currents of the Mind

In a boat made of thoughts, we drift and sway,
Chasing fish who giggle and play.
A seagull sneezes, and it starts to rain,
We paddle faster, but it's all in vain.

Thoughts like jellyfish, float here and there,
Wiggling and jiggling without a care.
A crab plays poker with a clam so sly,
As dolphins dance laughing, oh me, oh my!

Oars made of wishes, we row with glee,
Finding treasures in the depths of our spree.
"Is that a mermaid?" someone shouts with delight,
Only to find it's a cat in the moonlight.

From shores of nonsense, we sail away,
Chasing giggles until the end of the day.
In whirlpools of laughter, we spin around,
As waves of humor crash down, unbound.

Saline Secrets

Seashells whisper secrets, sandy and grand,
Of pirates who danced with a ticklish hand.
A shrimp in a tux, oh what a sight,
Swings his tiny legs, ready for a night.

The ocean's a jester, tickling the sand,
Making sandcastles no one can stand.
A fish wearing glasses, reading the news,
While a turtle snores in some pink fuzzy shoes.

With salty confessions, the waves start to giggle,
As fish in bow ties begin to wiggle.
A dolphin juggles pearls with all of his might,
While a crab tells a joke that's just out of sight.

Secrets of saltwater whisper and sing,
Of the wacky adventures that laughter can bring.
So next time you wander along the wet shore,
Listen for giggles, they echo and roar!

Blue Horizon Dreams

In dreams painted blue, the horizon calls,
With jellybean clouds and candyland falls.
A whale hums a tune, upbeat and spry,
As seagulls perform the cha-cha nearby.

The sun wears a hat, all floppy and wide,
While crabs play limbo, on the tide they glide.
A fish on a skateboard zooms past with flair,
Chasing a wave but without any care.

Dreams dance around like children at play,
With colors so vivid, they fly away.
The moon joins in, with a wink and a grin,
While starfish cheer loudly, "Let the fun begin!"

Painting the sky with giggles galore,
In dreams of the ocean, who could ask for more?
With laughter like bubbles that rise and then pop,
We float through our dreams, never wanting to stop.

The Stillness Beneath

Beneath the calm surface, the laughter flows,
As fish have a party in their stylish clothes.
A clam serves soup while a starfish sings,
With bubbles of joy, oh the fun that brings!

Seaweed dancers twist in a wiggly spree,
Twinkling like stars, a sight to see.
A log flume of giggles cascades from the rocks,
As jellyfish jump like they're wearing socks.

The stillness hides antics, in waves of delight,
As crabs tell tall tales by the pale moonlight.
A shark in a tux steps onto the scene,
Winks at a mermaid, so sly and keen.

Beneath the calm surface, we find a parade,
With banners of laughter that can't ever fade.
So dive into stillness, where humor can thrive,
In the depths of the ocean, we're truly alive!

Shimmers of the Celestial Tide

Dancing on waves, the seagulls play,
Their shadows twist in a silly ballet.
A crab with a hat, oh what a sight,
Scuttles away, filled with delight.

Sandcastles rise like dreams made of gold,
While kids yell out, their laughter unfolds.
Splashing in pools, they giggle with glee,
As fish toss their scales, a playful spree.

Drifting like clouds, our worries unfasten,
With palm trees swaying, the sea's our passion.
The tide rolls in, and we dance in the foam,
Each wave a giggle, our salty home.

Oh, the moon winks, creating the show,
As jellyfish glow with a soft, warm glow.
In this oceanic circus, we cheer,
With laughter and winks, we'll stay right here.

Secrets in the Salted Air

Whispers on breezes, secrets they share,
Beneath the wide sky, we hang without care.
A pelican dives, the splash is so grand,
While dolphins do tricks, like they planned.

Shells tell stories of days long gone,
Each a treasure, or maybe a con.
Sandy footprints lead to nowhere, it seems,
As crabs roll their eyes, and plot with dreams.

Surfers in stripes lean back on their boards,
While jellyfish dance to the ocean's chords.
A wave tips its hat, while seagulls do prance,
Life's one big joke, let's join in the dance.

With fizzy drinks and snacks in our hand,
We toast to the tides, our merry band.
In the salted air, with a chuckle and cheer,
Every ocean secret, we hold ever dear.

The Lullaby of Breaking Surf

Crashing and laughing, the surf sings a tune,
Like playful puppies under the moon.
Each wave is a whisper, or maybe a yawn,
As clams sit around, debating the dawn.

Starfish in flip-flops, what do they say?
"Let's grab some sunscreen; it's a beachy day!"
The tide rolls like laughter, steady and bright,
As pelicans plunge with all of their might.

Bubbles and giggles rise up from the sand,
Where the surf tells tales, oh so unplanned.
Seashells conspire, giggling their tales,
While the ocean winks, with its frothy veils.

At sunset, the sky wears its glittering best,
As we sit, full of snacks, and take a long rest.
With the lullaby soft and the world bathed in cheer,
The surf rocks us gently, while dreams drift near.

Tides of Memory and Mist

Waves toss and turn, like thoughts in our mind,
Dragging old memories, some silly, some kind.
A starfish with glasses reads a good book,
While octopuses plan a surprise hook.

The tide shifts and giggles, whispers in mist,
As clowns in the surf wave and twist.
A sandman appears, with a grin wide and bright,
While gulls shout a joke that takes flight.

With piña coladas, we bask on the shore,
Sharing silly secrets, and laughing some more.
Seagulls in tuxedos strut with great flair,
Inviting us all to dance in the air.

So here's to the tides, with their playful parade,
The memories made, like sandcastles laid.
In mist and in laughter, we'll write our own tale,
With the sea as our witness, we'll set our sails.

Murmurs from the Abyss

Bubbles rise with gossip light,
Deep in waters, what a sight!
Fish exchange their silly tales,
Of lost socks and floating snails.

A crab in dance, a shrimp in glee,
Found his groove, just wait and see!
Octopuses play hide and seek,
With squids that squirt and giggles peak.

Each wave a chuckle, each splash a cheer,
Oh, the joy when fish appear!
But beware the silly seaweed sways,
Entangling feet in playful ways!

So when you dip your toes to play,
Listen close, they'll laugh all day!
Join the fun, embrace the scene,
In the depths where laughter's keen.

Fleeting Reflections in the Dusk

As sun dips low, the shadows stretch,
A goldfish tells a fishy sketch.
His tales of a cat, so sly and spry,
With pounce and bounce, oh my, oh my!

Seashells gossip, listen near,
They've heard the whispers, they're all here!
With laughter echoing in the brine,
"Who wore that outfit? It's quite divine!"

A dolphin leaps with grace and flair,
"Did you see my triple backflip air?"
But oops! He lands with a splash so grand,
Now he's wearing seaweed like a band.

As dusk settles, the giggles flow,
In aquatic realms, they steal the show.
With mirrors of water, all spirits gleam,
In this twilight of fun, they collectively beam.

Chasing Shadows on the High Tide

Upon the crest of boisterous waves,
A sea otter plays, and misbehaves.
Rolling logs once stiff and straight,
Now splashed with giggles, they can't wait!

Seagulls squawk their rooftop news,
"Party in the surf, bring your blues!"
With combs and hats and snacks galore,
Under the sun, they dance on the shore.

The surfboards wobble, toes fly high,
A splash! A crash! Oh my, oh my!
They chase the light, crack jokes with glee,
Tidal truths like slippery sea.

"What's the secret to the ocean's sway?"
A fish replies, "Just play all day!"
With laughter bubbling, tides will tease,
In waters wide, they float with ease.

Beneath the Weave of Starlit Waters

Beneath the stars, where currents twine,
A fishy choir begins to shine.
"Did you hear the clam's last joke?"
Its punchline made the ocean choke!

Jellyfish float with grace so bright,
In rhythmic moves, they gleefully write.
Squiggle and squirm, they dance in pairs,
With laughter floating in gentle airs.

The sea cucumbers form a line,
To tell tales of their grand design.
"Who needs legs when you can glide?"
They chuckle softly, full of pride.

So come on down to the starlit scene,
Where laughter bubbles, pure and keen.
In every swirl, joy finds its way,
In watery depths, where dolphins play!

A Tide's Promise to the Sorrowful Shore

The sea's a joker, splashing my feet,
With every high tide, I dance to its beat.
It whispers secrets, tickles my toes,
While seagulls laugh at my silly woes.

With foam on my face, I giggle and scream,
As the waves throw back my sandcastle dream.
Each wave a prank, the ocean's sly jest,
I chase them back like a poorly-dressed guest.

The shore rolls its eyes, all sandy and wet,
As I trip on a shell, my own little threat.
Oh, how the tide makes a fool out of me,
But I laugh and I splatter, wild and free!

One day I'll conquer, but not today,
For laughter with tides is the silliest play.
The sea keeps its promise, though I may fall,
It cradles my heart, and that's best of all.

Dances of Light in the Abyssal Blue

In water so deep, where the fish do a jig,
A dolphin's flip ends in a giggling wig.
With bubbles around, we twirl in delight,
Oh, what a scene, just dancing with light!

The clam holds a party, all shells have a cheer,
As crabs do the cha-cha, they show no fear.
Bright sunbeams descend, a shimmering wave,
Lighting up scenes that no one could save.

A jellyfish joins, with a wiggle so grand,
Its tentacles sway as it takes to the sand.
We sway to the rhythm of currents and tides,
With laughter and bubbles, the fun never hides.

As the half-light begins to make shadows poke,
These dances of light aren't just a joke.
In the depths of the blue, we'll forever prance,
For life is a dance, a merry sea dance!

Ebbing Echoes

The waves come and go like a cheeky friend,
Whispering secrets at every bend.
They tug at my heart, then dash it away,
Oh silly sea, you're a jester at play!

With every retreat, I grip grain and sigh,
Oh tide, don't abandon, just give it a try!
But back it lurches, with a splish and a splash,
I laugh as it covers my toes in a flash.

Footprints are mere jokes, washed out of sight,
The ocean laughs loudly, as day turns to night.
It's a game of tag, and I'm always "it",
Chasing echoes of laughter, never to quit.

As I turn to leave, the tide makes a dash,
Just like a prankster, it goes with a splash.
My heart in the ocean, forever within,
With ebbing echoes, let the giggles begin!

Whispering Waves

The waves wear a grin, as they rise and they fall,
They tease with their shush, oh isn't that all?
They murmur sweet nothings to the sea foam,
Inviting me over, to be part of the roam.

They call out my name, a splashy parade,
Each glimmering crest, a prank they've conveyed.
With each little chuckle, I'm swept back and forth,
From this watery merry-go-round of mirth.

In bubbles of laughter, they carry my cheer,
Singing the stories only I can hear.
With a wink and a nod, they sweep me along,
In this funny ballet, where all dreams belong.

As the sun dips low, and colors ignite,
The waves keep whispering, oh what a sight!
With laughter and joy, forever they stay,
In the morning light of their playful display.

Serene Swells

Waves come crashing, oh what a sight,
Seaweed dances, a jellyfish flight.
Seagulls squawk, they drop their fries,
While dolphins giggle and make funny pies.

The tide retreats with a mighty roar,
Crabs do the cha-cha right on the shore.
A starfish yawns, takes a long, deep nap,
Funny how sea life can be in a flap.

Whales in tuxedos, they waltz and spin,
With clams in bow ties that join in the din.
Oysters giggle, pearls shine with glee,
In this aquatic world, oh what a spree!

So next time you visit the sunny beach,
Remember to laugh, let the waves teach.
For in the frolic of salt and foam,
Life's little quirks feel just like home.

In the Heart of the Sea

In the ocean deep, a fish told a joke,
A pufferfish giggled, then it almost choked.
Octopuses jive with eight different moves,
While crabs do the worm, and it really grooves!

A mermaid sings with a voice like a bell,
Her seashells giggle; they know her well.
They whisper secrets in the turquoise blue,
Of seaweed parties that you never knew.

The dolphins play tag, they're quick on their fins,
While turtles slow dance, letting the fun begin.
Starfish clap along, they never feel shy,
As waves keep the beat under the sky.

So take a dive where the laughter flows,
Join in the fun where the ocean glows.
For in the heart of this liquid charm,
The joy is infectious, there's no harm!

Silken Stirrings

In currents so smooth, the seaweed sways,
Anemones laugh through the bright sunny days.
Clownfish tell tales with a flick and a swirl,
Oh, the ocean's charm makes my head whirl!

A clam cracks a pun, and he's quite the chap,
While mussels join in with a snappy clap.
Barnacles gossip on rocks by the shore,
In this watery world, who could ask for more?

Bubbles are giggling, they pop with a flair,
And otters roll over without a care.
Sea cucumbers wiggle, all silly and spry,
Making waves of laughter as they drift by.

So dip your toes where the silliness gleams,
In the shimmering tides, dance out your dreams.
For in the lush waves of the ocean's embrace,
You'll find joy and laughter, a happy place.

Celestial Currents

Stars wink above, while the waves play along,
With flippers and fins, they sing a sweet song.
Constellations chuckle, lighting up the sea,
While lighthearted fish swim in pure glee.

An otter wearing shades slides down a log,
He splashes the seals with a playful smog.
Moonbeams dance softly, as comets streak by,
Drawing smiles from starfish, who giggle and sigh.

In deep cobalt pools, the laughter ignites,
With jellybeans jiving under silvery lights.
A whale tells tall tales of ships long ago,
As the ocean keeps chuckling, gently aglow.

So sail on the waves of this cosmic delight,
Where every splash sends the stars into flight.
In the cosmic waters, let your worries cease,
For laughter unites us, bringing joy and peace.

Water's Embrace

In a puddle, a dog did leap,
Waves of splashes, splish and beep.
Frogs in chorus, croak and croak,
Tickled toes, oh, what a joke!

A fish flopped out, quite the show,
Dancing on grass, oh, where to go?
Slick and slimy, a slippery slide,
Giggling neighbors, all in stride.

A splash here, a splash there,
Water balloons fly through the air!
The sunbeam laughs, a bright charade,
As kids in puddles, their worries fade.

Finally, the hose sprays wide,
Chasing laughter, can't help but glide.
In the fountain, a duck does quack,
Water's embrace, we won't look back.

Starlit Waves

Under the moon, sea foam does swirl,
Mermaids giggle, giving a twirl.
Starfish play cards, with shells for stakes,
While crabs do tango, making mistakes.

The lighthouse beams, a disco light,
Fish in tuxedos dancing at night.
Octopuses juggle, in rhythmic sway,
Each plop and splash, a grand cabaret!

A seagull swoops, with a cheeky dive,
Wind in feathers, oh, how they thrive.
With ice cream cones, they make a mess,
Sticky paws in this starlit dress.

The waves giggle, a bubbly sound,
As shells tell stories from the ground.
So raise a shell to evening's delight,
For in this place, all wrongs feel right.

Layers of Liquid Dreams

A teacup spills, a whirlpool forms,
In sugar, chaos, a battle of storms.
Lemon's zesty twist, a capricious friend,
As laughter bubbles, on fun we depend.

Jellyfish in hats, float by with grace,
While dolphins play hopscotch, not a trace.
A turtle in goggles swims with style,
In this great ocean, let's linger awhile.

Goldfish skate with splashes galore,
While pirate parrots squawk, "Bring me more!"
Waves crash with giggles, a swirling spree,
In this liquid dream, we're all fancy-free.

With splashes of color, the sea's a canvas,
Each drop a laugh, let's all be the braves.
So fill up your cups, let's toast this theme,
To layers of laughter, and wildest dreams!

Turbulent Thoughts

A waterfall thunders, thoughts go splash,
In the pond, silly frogs take a crash.
Clowns in kayaks, pelting with pies,
Waterlogged plans, oh, what a surprise!

Swirling whirlpools, a raucous dance,
Each wave a quirk, inviting chance.
Fish in tuxedos swap tales of woe,
While dolphins leap high, putting on a show.

A little duckling, so out of sync,
Paddles in circles, and starts to think.
Don't take life too serious, let's cheer,
In this crazy lake, there's nothing to fear!

So kick off your shoes, let's frolic about,
Dip our toes in, let go of doubt.
Amongst the bubbles, let spirits soar,
In this tidal jester, we laugh evermore.

Refracted Radiance

Sunlight dances on the waves,
A fish jumps, steals a snack,
I chuckle as it flips and sways,
Splash! It's gone, just like that.

Seagulls squawk in feathered glee,
Diving down for unexpected treats,
One lands on my head, oh, whee!
Now I'm the pirate with bird greets.

Crabs in coats of vibrant hue,
Slide sideways with a silly prance,
I can't help but laugh, it's true,
Nature's got the best of dance!

A beach ball bounces, what a sight,
It rolls away, a comical quest,
Chasing it feels just so right,
Who knew fun could be such a test?

Overture of the Ocean

The ocean sings a quirky tune,
With bubbles popping, sounds galore,
Dance along beneath the moon,
Jellyfish zoom, what's it for?

Crustaceans jam with shells in tow,
A conga line near the shore,
Bouncing and tumbling, steal the show,
Hey! Crabby dancers, give me more!

Waves giggle as they crash and play,
They wave back, now isn't that wild?
And just like kids on a sunny day,
Wave fights begin, every adult a child.

A tide pool party, oh what fun,
Starfish stick around for some laughs,
Their spindly arms in unison,
Who knew sea life had such gaffes?

Whispers in the Wind

Winds carry secrets, oh so sly,
A whisper here, a giggle near,
Waves catch on with a soft reply,
"Did you see that? I need a beer!"

A dolphin jumps, looks proud and bright,
It looks at me with a cheeky grin,
"Catch me if you can, you'll lose the light,"
And with a splash, it's off to spin.

The breeze kicks up, a whirlwind tease,
As my hat flies off, oh, where it lands?
A flock of gulls takes it with ease,
I'll join them next time - gulls have plans!

Sandcastles crumble with a clink,
What a sight, as laughter unfolds,
Just like a drink that's past the brink,
These beach antics never grow old.

Secrets of the Surface

Bubbles rise with giddy glee,
Each one holds a silly tale,
What's that beast peeking at me?
A friendly fish with a big, bright scale!

Underneath, the dance of lights,
Fins flutter like cards in a game,
Turtles play hide and seek in sights,
And I'm the only one to blame!

A lazy seal rests on a rock,
It snores loudly, quite the show,
"Excuse me, sir, is that your clock?"
Its flipper waves, then off it goes!

The tide pulls back to start again,
A squishy ball rolls my way,
I chase it down with ocean's zen,
Who knew the sea could be so play?

Cascading Reverberations

A fish wore a hat on its head,
It danced to the waves, full of dread.
It slipped on a seaweed slice,
And yelled, 'Oh, this isn't nice!'

A crab took a sip of some tea,
In a shell, he felt fancy and free.
A seagull squawked down from the sky,
'You look like a fool!' it did cry.

A whale made a splash quite profound,
With laughter that boomed all around.
The fish in its hat gave a twist,
And thought, 'How did I get in this mess?'

With bubbles and giggles they rolled,
The ocean was laughing, behold!
In a swirl like a merry parade,
The hilarity just wouldn't fade.

Shores of Memory

The gulls were gossiping, quite absurd,
About the shrimp who lost his third word.
He stuttered and stammered, oh so bright,
'Incredible, truly, what a sight!'

A hermit crab scuttled, dressed like a knight,
Declaring his castle with sheer delight.
But slipping on sand, he soon lost pride,
Cried, 'I need a moat for my tide!'

Starfish were plotting a dance off,
While the octopus said, 'Woo, that's a scoff!'
They twisted and twirled with sheer flair,
Until one got tangled in seaweed hair.

Then the dolphins decided to play,
They leaped 'round like children at play.
With splashes and laughter, they cheered,
In shores of memory, fun appeared.

Confluence of Selves

In a bubble, a crab saw his face,
He shouted, 'This isn't my place!'
With claws at the ready, he waved,
'Let's all go home, I'm quite knave!'

The jellyfish floated like a balloon,
Singing off-key a humorous tune.
'I'm so transparent,' he gave a grin,
'I'll float through your life with a spin!'

A clam snapped its shell, oh so proud,
'Take a look at my pearl — it's allowed!'
But the oyster replied with a wink,
'It's nothing but sand, let me think.'

They laughed till the tide turned to night,
For the confluence was sheer delight.
With smiles wide and hearts full of glee,
They forged new selves in the sea.

Salty Serenades

Octopus strummed on a seashell guitar,
Singing 'bout life in the salty bazaar.
Though the fish tried to dance, it was quite a flop,
Whirling round and round till they did plop!

Turtles doing the cha-cha on sand,
With moves so silly, it's quite unplanned.
The wind joined in with a whoosh and a blow,
While laughter erupted from head to toe.

The dolphins slid down waves like slick slides,
Chasing each other in bubbly rides.
With flips and tricks under the sun's ray,
They turned every moment into a play.

With salt in the air and joy all around,
The ocean's sweet music can truly astound.
Together, they soared with the tide and the breeze,
Creating serenades that brought them to ease.

www.ingramcontent.com/pod-product-compliance
Lightning Source LLC
Chambersburg PA
CBHW062111280426
43661CB00086B/454